Free Verse Editions
Edited by Jon Thompson

DAY IN, DAY OUT

LONDON • GLASGOW • LOS ANGELES •
LA JOLLA • VANCOUVER • MANHATTAN • BROOKLYN

Simon Smith

Parlor Press
Anderson, South Carolina
www.parlorpress.com

Parlor Press LLC, Anderson, South Carolina, 29621

Printed in the United States of America
S A N: 2 5 4 - 8 8 7 9

Library of Congress Cataloging-in-Publication Data on File

978-1-60235-396-1 (paperback)
978-1-60235-407-4 (PDF)
978-1-60235-410-4 (ePub)

1 2 3 4 5

Cover design by David Blakesley.
Cover image: You, no 11 (detail) by Felicity Allen, 2016,
    watercolour on paper. Reproduced by permission of the
    artist. © Felicity Allen.
Printed on acid-free paper.

Parlor Press, LLC is an independent publisher of scholarly and
trade titles in print and multimedia formats. This book is available
in paperback and ebook formats from Parlor Press on the World
Wide Web at http://www.parlorpress.com or through online and
brick-and-mortar bookstores. For submission information or to
find out about Parlor Press publications, write to Parlor Press,
3015 Brackenberry Drive, Anderson, South Carolina, 29621, or
email editor@parlorpress.com.

*To Felicity Allen and
in memory of my father, Christopher Smith*

Contents

Contents

ZEROSEVEN *61*

26 POEMS: CALIFORNIALAND IN WINTER *69*

Contents

THE F TRAIN *111*

Contents

Acknowledgments

Day In, Day Out is a sequence of poetry journals. The volume brings together sequences, spanning the period between 11 April 2012 and 27 June 2014.

Some of these poems previously appeared in: *Cordite*; *First Offense*; *Free Verse: A Journal of Contemporary Poetry & Poetics*; *Molly Bloom*; *Shearsman Magazine*; *Veer Journal 4: Veer Vier: for Will Rowe*; and, *ZONE*. I offer my grateful thanks to those editors for their attention and patience.

Many thanks to The University of Kent, which gave me research leave from January to June 2014 when half of these poems were written.

This book is dedicated to Felicity Allen, and is in memory of my father, Christopher Smith, 27.xi.1932-19.i.2014.

Day In, Day Out

ZEROFOURZEROFIVEZEROSIXTWENTYTWELVE

(2012)

Airlane Avenue

'a brisk twenty knots from the south west,' the captain sez on

touch down we're released from Beavis & Butthead, F53 & 54

pile luggage in the Scion – bodies too

consciousness dumped beside, ten minutes, then Airlane Avenue
and Thai food

Flick teaching Milena republicanism versus monarchism

tin of commemorative shortbread in one hand, Queen's Diamond
Jubilee mug
in the other

Béatrice sez: 'orange chicken' and 'you're standing in the freezer/
ice-box'

from where I'm not sure if this is California or London

astride the San Andreas Fault

or not off to the east and the desert out to Joshua Tree and Palm
Springs

I'm thinking I'm reading

Sixpack 7/8 Paul Blackburn Issue

and proofs of *Twenty-five Catvllvs* for Kelvin and Ian

Béatrice sez: SepulVEda

12/4/12

dawn chorus at six

                        grey

light fading to grey-blue

tea

      and/or coffee

pending credit card details and Rent-A-Wreck, the key to

a silver Hyundai Accent sedan, license plate 4PJA659, this time,

and a half tank of gas

a trip over the Painted Hills (calling for more regular) to Roughley
    Manor

                                     (no you couldn't

make it up   165 miles due

east of LA on I-60 East

Twentynine Palms

Dick Dale its most famous resident, Wikipedia sez

                      'Misirlou' (with the Del Tones) 1963

and the biggest U.S. military base in the World training for desert
    operations

'I-RACK'   Operation Desert Storm

the 'Third World Man' 'he's been mobilized since dawn'

his lawn sprinkler reveille at zero five thirty

US Marine Corps cheek by jowl with 'leezur'

Friday, Thirteenth

I write today's poem tomorrow

stolen from yesterday's memory:

gophers, small lizards, no sign

of rattlesnakes, coyotes or kingsnakes

but I know they're there

various familiar unidentified cacti

just flowering pinks, yellows, reds more-than-alive

in expectation of a Spring downpour

a pair of hawks rising at Split Rock

Gram Parsons' 'Love Hurts' on the iPhone

a head full of UFOs and LSD

                              dead at Joshua Tree

nineteenth September nineteen seventy-three

through rainstorms on eye ten and eye one ten

flashing back: unexpected exploding pick-up on I-60

haul across the desert

we occupy THE INNER EMPIRE K-CAL 9 Weather informs us

with a chance of snow above 5,500 feet   and storms after midday
    with rainfall

of one to two inches

then home for Guy's pasta and conversation

a couple of fine pale ales, a good red wine

4/14/12

Cruising down Vista del Mar

Guy at the wheel of his scarlet-immaculate '88 Mercedes 560 SL
    coupe

the dream car of dreams glides by as long as a freeway

English boy's dream

come true past Manhattan Beach towards Hermosa

via Hyperion Way and the oil refinery

a stroll on the pier and a pair of smoothies

'one banana and pineapple (with apple juice) for this man

one strawberry (with soya milk) for this man, please,'

and 'which way to Hawaii,' we ask the pilot

Venice Beach

First: drive down to Marina del Rey

turn right, a blue surfer shark will greet you, tell his story for a nickel

my nickel, I pick out

New Collected Poems (with CD of the poet reading) by George Oppen

and Garry Thomas Morse, *After Jack* at Small World Books

Béatrice selects a memoir and an Anne Tyler novel,

and from the Vietnamese hat stall, a fine, new sun bonnet for Flick

the endless posé of Harley's, the odd

Kawa, and clichéd pick ups – Ford   Toyota   GMC

heading east

WRONG WAY

DO NOT ENTER

Horizon Ave.

it sez

Lunch: ordered off of the menu at Mao's Kitchen –

'Chinese country cooking with Red Memories,' 'Lunch Combination
for the Masses'

"Mao loved to say, "Wei renmin fuwu!" – "Serve the people!""

Mao is vegan friendly, it sez.

Home: to Airlane Avenue after a detour to Ralph's for trash bags

a bourbon and run through Guy's machine code poems

11781 W. Sunset Blvd. (reprise)

Return to Apartment # 34

driving the hire car – a simple metal box –

whilst reading Jeff Clark's *Arab Rab* in the other hand

waiting for my Maruchan Instant Lunch (Chicken Flavor)

to metamorphosise from dust

with its zero per cent Trans Fat

and the U.S. Marine Corps

colonel in my memory of Hué

alights without a scratch

his Bell Huey chopper stirs the dirt

'do you know who you're talking to? Do ya?' The man sez

which proves I'm writing like a sophomore

and the more you find out the less you understand

04/17/12

Trip to Bank of America on San Vicente

$200 from the ATM, then down Barrington

right at Olympic

Trader Joe's for groceries

pick a Zinfandel from the Alexander Valley for later, my choice simply

the name: Rendition

Later still: cross Sunset to the Angelino

rise to the 17th Floor, meet

Flick and Toby for cocktails

gazing across I-405 I drive through air

to the horizon and the 'off'

ramp reaching out   the Ocean

'and close your eyes with holy dread'

Seeing stars in the night I've found

I dreamt up the title of my 'occasional poems,'

On the Road to Xanadu

crossing the 't's'

        go on, drive thru

the freeways of Paradise Guy Bennett, we love you.

4/19/12

fill the tank with $40 of regular on Sepulveda

meeting Flick off the monorail at The Getty

then down to La Jolla two and a half hours of Interstate

405 merging right into I-5

Rest Area 'under construction'

to arise on the terrace at Ellentown Road

sipping martini facing a chilly westerly

off the endless Pacific

one late afternoon hang-glider

rises from the headland

day-glo yellow sail

mistaken for picnic table canopy

then three more monstrous

off the sandstone cliffs

scoops of ice-cream, pistachio,

strawberry, orange sorbet then a fourth

and a red-shouldered hawk or peregrine

surfers freeze Black's Beach

below a sky broadening a bluer blue

Poem with a Line Altered from a Translation by Paul Blackburn

built on a Yuman burial site

Cherokee, Warrior, Raptor – a drive full

white pick ups – Trader Joe, GI

Joe, 'leez-ur'-time-Joe

Horizon Way leads to Ellentown Road

sandstone or sand

prone to unstable slippage bones

and skulls with each landslide

the burials flexed

crouching to return

to where they were the seventeen

exhumations 2,000 years at least

one skull carbon-dated

6,700 years in the sand

then stone

a healthy diet of seafood and land vegetation

two week cliff inspections by Coastguard chopper

searching for the signs

and how the rich conduct

their business in our heads

North Star straight flood through the plate glass and memory

of the last meal, a six inch Subway – ham, Swiss cheese, pickle,
    mustard, mayo

at the gate a sacred place   and the last

                    STOP sign before Japan

International Date Line

La Jolla fog-bound looking over the cliff

to 30 or 40 cormorants bobbing up

and down Pacific surf

behind the wheel of the Accent GL, 12.49pm

north on I-5 miss

the turn for I-405, so carry

on the I-5, across east

to west on I-22 to meet the 405 again

drop away to Manchester

Avenue et voilà the door to Guy and Béatrice's, 8128 Airlane
    Avenue 3.47pm

check the hire car's over-active air con. Check.

Talk and beer, cheese, fresh pineapple, more talk LAX

on time. Check-in on time. Departure to Heathrow. On time.

Taxi 3.16 pm London, 7.16 am LA.

copies of *or* Issue Eight line my suitcase

'Ode: Sat Nav Narrative on Flying into LAX'

'Los Angeles River'

'Eyewitness News'

'Paradise Cove'

        — included

a full run (1-8) for the Poetry Library, London

Two Days Old

two days ago

this was the lo-fi solution

choose the right

book for my flight (Blackburn's *Proensa*? Guy's *Last Words*) – it's the
   grief

of ending

the journey I feel

the grief   sipping Mongoose still @ 38,000 ft in the Surma,
   Dulwich

a TV chef's endorsement beams away from the wall

comfort food for missing

a wife   this-day-of-our-Lord

twenty-second-of-April-two-thousand-&-twelve

imagining as far west as the west will be imagined

                            for sir's palate

a little heavy red

           oh, its oh two forty-two am in London

the evening has just begun my body sez

Twenty-Three-Oh-Four-Twelve

David's b/day

a BIG five by a BIG two

my head as far west as the western rim   by proxy
    intelligent

pictures by Françoise Gilot slipping

down the cliff out

of memory and the Pacific

clam stones   fossil shark's tooth   rolled stone tools
    the midden

what you forgot at the petrol station –

                      the pint

of homogenised milk, a symbol

                    of our Time   blue
chip

of paint adheres to a cotton shirt

and all the trained resources in the World build pressure

behind the purchase   my
    new iPhone 4S

has 'historical status' and is 'out

for delivery'   the web site updates my role

sharp as is   required at interview

24/4/12

Shakespeare's b/day yesterday's news

                                         uncertain myths perpetuated

time enough   to field questions   deflect your glare

for the sake of the password do you place numbers or letters first?

I'm a numbers man myself

Some days it just doesn't happen.

This is one of those days.

NFT

a sandwich (ham and egg) at the NT snack bar passing through

to the Glad three o'clock and Mr David Rees

Barrier Man in black nylon jacket scraping around barriers

three pints of San Miguel ticks some boxes and filthy weather

Boot & Flogger for white port and soda

cab it up town to curry   the Halal since 1939

Canterbury Tales

V40 @ 2,700 RPM icy white against the gloom

                                            reaction time

lapsed to three

second

delay aqua

                plane the long drag waterlogged   all the way up

Chatham   Gravesend

beyond

                 eight hours in the office,

turn around, home

                     fifty-eight miles each way by 'later'

hangs a speech

bubble above

pork belly, Vivaldi

                    new potatoes, sautèd cabbage leaves for dinner

I imagine the Pacific swell below

& listen to Radio 4's nine o'clock bulletin   [fall asleep]

conscious suddenly nine twenty pm

                                        jet-lag dissolves into sleep

Rehearsal

start late: 11.30, Sam's place

Matt set up, David

arrives with his poem, me with mine

'Constellation'

        Evan later

new tenor, with a passing acquaintance

record   sample   rehearse   re-
record 'Constellation'

chaffinch and gull   chirrup and cry

        snuck in their chat

                @4.30

a two hour drive to Essex, *Miles in the Sky*, then migraine on the
    twenty-five no

focus to the left

eye

peripheral   cocktail of lack

of sleep and jet-lag

                    driving

my mother's neatly cut two rounds of sandwiches

cheese and pickle   eyesight

back, memories to school   packed lunch,
   the squares neat

folded into grey

grease-proof paper   times

ten years into how many

                                        lemon-sole, one

Sauvignon, one Chardonnay and chat for now   Burt

Bacharach, on BBC 4, 'the look of love,' nineteen-sixty-

eight lives forever

Letter, Yesterday's: with a Poem Attached by Paul Blackburn, & my Entry for the Day Before Yesterday

email takes the place of my letters today

today's entry is reflection

and daily account

to cheer you along

yes, Evan clicked at keys and stops in step to the mouthings

Matt sampled then re-processed

as David and I

spoke line into line

each layer broadcast above

the other   cut

my nose shaving invisible

beneath my left nostril

sore with the cologne, this morning

stings recall

Joshua Tree, Split Rock, the exit for Palm Springs

the downpour as we skimmed Riverside

Paul Blackburn wrote   the desert —

'Along the San Andreas Fault'

The neon donuts blink   .   *Other*

side of the mountains / yr in the desert   .   *Here*

you really know it   .   *Barry*

Goldwater, Jr. is Congressman

these are his people   .

lines and stanzas

                 hang   mobile

hang-gliders in air   on electronic

ether

                               the immense

and silent   S   P   A   C   E   S

       between

us

           a very personal poem

to drop

      kisses into

           browsing data and love

Rain

                    RAIN   RAIN   RAIN   the May

blossom beaten into the earth, no Ezra

Pound about to transcend the experience

with a nuclear

                    alchemy, no *Métro*, no wet

black bough, no faces

only petals, simple   pink-blue petals   beaten, muddy petals

Miles

from the train   bleak streets of Tonbridge

      the weeds luminous at seven-forty

last night

land-line down – mobile hot with incoming calls and me

supposed to be meeting Rees   to drink and eat and meebee
    plot and a sharp

intake of breath narrowly missed

by a white Renault van close as my

body misses your body

listening to Miles, the sequence from *Filles De Kilimanjaro*   stuck

at *Bitches Brew*   where is

the body   the body we can't live

without miles   from you

a long way from Bebop that's where

Ode in the Shape of a Lament

'Early Signs Point to Second Term for Tory' – so four more years of
    Boris then –

fitting to a less than perfect twenty-four hours – ten years

since Keith's death – Dorothy in a terrible state – David's

now diagnosed diabetes – the phone line down – the Internet

down – no Skype for days – all in sympathy like a drooping flag

or colour – you 6,000 miles adrift, Miles

Davis' 'In A Silent Way/It's About That Time,' the only

consolation, and dreaming of Catullus

I return to Brandon Brown and the Zukofskys'

catch the 6.38 from Canterbury West not knowing

what we'll eat flying thru grey

dusk the Kent countryside translated into London Bridge

May Day

doze about four in the afternoon

more than habit the need

to lie down these past 30 years

each siesta

                    in the genes? Great

grandma's genes?

                    late afternoon, stopped for rest

the old lady sings her hymn to the streets again

and again perched on the front

garden wall –blue and white turban, bleached white dress

                              (but this is not Pentecost?)

the song upon her and the memory of home   randomly

chosen spot where she sees her God, one

withered leg behind one good one

things forever pass unknown

things forever past unknown   Sonny Rollins 'Swing

Low Sweet Chariot' duets from the stereo

meaning this poem is dedicated

to my wife today no more than a chilly 9 degrees   no sun
    grey and rain

and this the weekend ten years on from Keith's death, which

day we'll never know

Brooklyn-Manhattan Transit

feeling a dull tiredness except for the impossible burning sensation behind

my right ear – shingles? No.

Time for a check up, Tuesday? Yes. Elect to read

Blackburn's 'A Dull Poem (for L.Z.)' to kick

start my work on Catullus,

        then the street and 'waves of somewhere' else

              in the middle of

P.B.'s *Brooklyn-Manhattan Transit* from the Totem Press, New York, 1960,
              I look up

     '7.15' printed

in LED and the news: Sarkozy out Hollande in,

and the first French socialist president in 17 years.

A weekend of elections

Monday's Blues

Bank Holiday best sat out.

So I sit it out. Then what?

Bills, road tax the car, renew my driver's licence – fail

online: – announce *Feedback* on Facebook to virtual

and real underwhelming indifference

Is my 'star falling'? Did it ever ascend?

Quick recce to the supermarket. Bath. Radio 4. Skype down

Dot gone and her mother

                              I can hear

but not see her

she can see me

behind a blank wall of 6,500 miles   the virtual collapses the real

info into deception

a crow passing right past my bedroom window right there it was

sounds like a dog   sounds like a cat   sounds like a crow

in the end sounds like a crow   crow Doppler effect the moon passed the Earth closest tonight, since when

                              a big mooning face of a moon

at the empty bedroom

window

Greenwich Meridian

How am I going to fill these days

but with other days like today

this first of June

                         – a morning with Caroline

Smith talking about Flick, the con-

nection between women

artists closer

than first apparent or possibly

real, then chatting

away with Ian turns

out he knew Evan – did a programme for Radio

3   (years ago)   later

remove my glasses for short

distance vision, reading the Kindle, push

the glasses back to restore for long-distance

driving   looking at clouds

        this is seeing AGE

                         so the eighth of May

is this Friday seeing the first of June

'Fullset £10'

the sign sez

there's a dip in the weather (overcast, humid) sunny by four, freshened

scouring S.E. London for somewhere

                               to dwell, Forest

Hill, Deptford   (ghost of Kit Marlowe, violence to the
    geography – a myth

tobacco-smoking, atheist, pederast

unmarked grave four hundred and nineteen years ago yesterday marks

the occasion, 'great reckoning in a little room'

                             Surrey Quays, Rotherhithe

history of a river, source, origin

snakes between quays, tower blocks, cottages, power

house to Empire – long gone

the traffic heavy / slow along Lower Street, the neatly

manicured rose-beds of council estates

block after block of low-rise to the river front and docks –

now marina   tow path given over to cycle ways and pedestrian ginnel

Plough Way SE8 somewhere possible

checking in the day in free-form

first glass of Côtes du Rhône at six – served at room temperature

Jubilee

up midday

bathed, toweled dry

ignoring the Diamond

Jubilee only matched by lunchtime drivel from the monotone

Laureate droned out of the speaker

'what music would you choose for your funeral,'

chirps Michael Berkeley –'The Stripper' – sez it all

and all we need to know and all manner of things –

a lunch of cheese, humus, Melton Mowbray pie, salt, pepper, Dijon mustard,
                                                                    a glass of Fitou

read on: *The Cities*, thru

pouring rain and chill a thousand

ships, Helen the myth

launched them not 'our Queen

Elizabeth,' a pageant, not since 1662 . . . process

the River

            nostalgia for Dunkirk

                                    is, ahem, besides

which Blackburn, this daily falling in love

with the World itself and this falling daily

Begin Again

late morning in bed

reading / looking at *Begin Again*

surprise and delight at how you are made

of numerous portraits, a stranger to others

but the construct 'you' conjures your presence

the day I gave up drinking today

today and a walk abroad past the Orange Café

up Telegraph Hill Upper Park, across

Drakefell and the railway footbridge

along St Asaph's and Linden Grove

to enact our return over and over

talking   talking   talking

where do we live?   what do we inhabit?

what place // language the place of habitation

then to the supermarket, guess at what we might eat

a little chicken with pancetta, a cold glass of Badoit

Liz appears for tea   sit out in the garden

where are we going /

                    to live

kicked into the long grass alongside the 12K from ma and pa

The Queen's Speech

Time of year – external for Greenwich

a crate full and Beethoven

Opus 131 to keep me going

the small wee hours

then Mingus at the piano. Improv.

The old lady wails her elegy

I've lots of things to announce from my own front garden

and a chance to reflect *not* react.

Dinner. Pack for Glasgow and sleep

six hours, 'no go'

Blackburn's last words to his notebook

The Music of Sauchiehall Street

Pee – use the *courtesy*

hand wash supplied, the broken

down trains and carriages at Carnforth broke my heart, Virgin trains

to the north west and Glasgow, whipped past North Fell Garage, the M6
and Great North-West

line share the same valley, sliver of an inlet

at Morcambe Bay caravan park

buzzard wing-tip

feathers spread like fingers

fingers of the pool hall

expert wag about to put the eight ball

down   baize

to rain-heavy cloud   cloud down

over Scafell / Blencathra

dark blue / grey

        slopes to Wasdale

Coach D: Time 12:15 according to the Jenny Holzer LED

I make it 12:32

                running late after Carlisle

hardly anyone to Glasgow

Check in – the Argyll Hotel (actually the Argyll Guest House)

where I seem to have dragged that warbling car alarm five hundred miles

from home, watching Alec Baldwin and Kim Bassinger in the 1994 re-make
of *The Getaway*

Feedback

The 'Feedback' gig /

         then The-Quartet gig

later after dinner

at Deeson's

3.40 run thru / rehearsal

         we're all firing tight

tighten cues

         David and Matt especially

rain sheets down work is work and new / old Blackburn 'The Beau
    Fleuve Series
         Number One'

Three Dreams and an Old Poem

lining up the Zukofskys' *Catullus* for attention

the pocket biro (Porsche design knocking around lost a year

         no lost notebook held hostage

thru suspended time and circumstance and its precious content

voices held within   tenor voiced

Song Thrush

I go on a twenty-four hour holiday not to

disappear exactly

pause / fold / fault

in time awake at seven

drowse   not to rise 'til nine

then song thrush shows up

cappuccino and cocoa

bitter sprinkle, a Danish (custard

which won't lose me weight, the mountain

man at the next table needs cutting down to size

I'm drinking coffee with nothing better to do

and some irritation in the legs

paid up, the waitress

with all the charm has turned charm to 'off' – like a tap

next to Kelvingrove Park – a delight by daylight

looming menace and obstacle by night, reality

more complex than our (shared) continental idealisms

at 2.46 the rain comes down

this occasional journal – journal of occasion

stomach doing flip-flops and belly somersaults

Stravaigin's   strap line   mission statement   platitude

'think global eat/act local'   FEED THE WORLD

all the charm of a scratch card

the single malt clear and bonny as a bell though

the liquor store on Argyll Street

everything for sale

booze, sweets, gum, the lot

behind tough mesh and grill, how I imagine

Harlem or the Watts Project to be

without black people

                  to order my Red Stripe

a kind of protest (probably political) (emphasise the 'kind of')

its so difficult being away from home

wait for the rain and the rain comes

Days

BBC News 24 obliterates me like the Gulf Stream   overwhelming data

and nowhere to put it

                  Syria: so many /

too many tears upon the World

next:

              Eurozone Debt Crisis

who's to pay /

            new place to live

the thought starts up a fresh pattern anew

       a morning to wander

       the streets, down Sauchiehall,

       Hope, by Central Station popping

       into Waterstone's (without the apostrophe) then Ryman's

       (without the apostrophe) for a spring-bound file

       ahead of time . . .

pay up return the electronic key 10:30 sharp

a time to leave (good as any) The Argyll Hotel / Guest House meet F. from the London Express 12:01 (which arrives 12:06

all I want is to make your day

and add another to it

into a lifetime

but what's the rush

the rush of days is to come

Blackburn writing through the early hours

to keep himself

company knowing

death right there   a day full

gestures, rituals and no bad thing

Stan's Day

two floors up in The Heritage Hotel looking down

the red VW transforms into the grey one parked across the street

opposite London Plane trees furnish the Great West Road, Glasgow

a walk about the city

begins with a latte and Americano plus hot milk

then on to the MFA exhibition at the Glue Factory

back to the Rene Macintosh building of the GSA

and Stan's show where I buy a plaster avocado   a work of art

for Flick the perfect gift *I* think

then taxi back to the hotel

watch the Denmark / Holland upset

after dinner at Number 16

followed by a peaty malt

Heritage Hotel

walk to the Transport Museum beneath graphite skies

latte and a little water begin the day song

thrush turns up

drizzle no driving rain, browsing the exhibits

the history of my life through manufactured objects

Austin Mini (trips to Cornwall

Raleigh Chopper, the 'bubble' car, Beetle, Hillman

Imp

bridge across the Kelvin – herring gull dive-bombs a motionless heron

who sees it as it is

pulling out of Central Station

the estates of Motherwell

'cats don't lie,' the boy pleads from Seat 48

Coach D   parents on a hi

tea of Stella, poor white wine, bag of Quavers

film mimes from the lap-top Pixel-Disney mix

of cod-cute

directly to slasher movie

mine was a Mark 1, orange, my dad's whole week wage at £32.99,
                                                  and months of hardship

there's love and beyond Carlisle intermittent cloud and blue

note at high speed, speed of the atmosphere, speed of the weather

Monday's Blues (Part II)

wet drive to Ramsgate:

        drenched Paul Smith jacket sponging off wing-mirrors

the motorway cruise and 'The Today Programme' 'til 08:50 park the car
                                at Waitrose

three / four bed 140K / 170K

Regency / Victorian / Edwardian 'with period charm'

no coffee bar mentality to Ramsgate

a language you have to work hard with everyday:

the white Escort van in the rear view

mirror becomes the white Escort van

fifty yards down the middle lane

kicking up a saturated windscreen

road spray and torrential rain

more grease and grit than fresh

rainwater   now pre-match

analysis to the England / France kick-off

Hanson, Southgate   line up

pint-to-the-line of Asahi

watch the game with text commentary

England and France split the points

Leaving

after Henry's and Jan's leaving   CURRY

chutney, popadoms, red onion, something with tumeric

a large party of teenagers just finishing up at the Raj Venue

the good weather (at last) has brought people out

(must check the iPhone to see what's going on

a decent group of young people out to enjoy themselves

that is what they are

a few hours later / (decades earlier)

a madras and several Stellas up the road spread across Conrad's grave c.1979

Last Leg

keys found

house sale in shape, sun out, the half

caught look on the face, a sunny

day in Manchester 2:22 looks like my train

divvying up £3.50 a pint

of Amstel on Piccadilly Station *The Mayfield*

and Sky News, pint-to-line – BIG

question of the day – England to beat Ukraine?

already to Stockport   Stoke-on-Trent

Coach B quiet at 6 – clientele away from the bars

to watch the game

                                        The Lamb deserted

the German tourists rise, stretch, leave

after pub food at 5:30   tuning in –

'if it weren't for the midgets it'd be the perfect place to camp'

and '"Hemingway, 'an-y-way,'" two words with the same meaning.'

A thirty-spot and a pocket-full of change,

then, later: look up Berryman drowned in mud on Wikipedia

'we need something more than repeats of "Friends"'

Due North

note cctv cameras in operation (nearly scribble 'inspiration'

dozing out of Euston

flash thru Dumfries, past rivers' meanders

condensed orange juice bacon roll, tea. Train to Glasgow

(again).

               'Unity for Tyres,' the sign sez.

Fields' distances   from the Safety Glass, the window square

neat, safe and packaged

in Coolidge's book a Guston figure laid out, reclining

               background, gorse, perfect

             red van occupies the landscape

Allen Fisher / *PLACE*

holed up for the day at Royal Holloway,

                                        talking about

and talking to Allen Fisher / no word

on Cavendish Street, yet the deal

busted (it seems) on our building's

insurance, all bets are off

re-group, take stock

the place I find is Fisher's *PLACE*

the death throes of *SPUTTER* in the quest for cobalt blue

pictures in /

                to text

the 'we' of utterance, place

in the function /

                action of the text

Blake as maker in the facture

Travelodge

third trip north in ten days

                              Bolton, egg and spinach sandwich

(lunch) free range, a green tea

the 747 above emits the same wail as Mingus' 'Ecclusiastics' on the head
set

you believe in lists to, from and about a crisis

as the property deal falls flat on its face and about our ears

as the house itself collapses, like collapsed

data – edgy, on edge

> *this poem is a suspicious item on its way*
>
> *to Manchester Piccadilly and should be reported*
>
> *to the police as we pull into Stoke-on-Trent*
>
> *this eighteenth day of June two thousand and twelve*

listening to 'ROTE/THRU' this other side

of composition a lyric collapsing /

                                        a lyrical collapsing
in on itself, folding over

The Sims come to mind

repellent in its extreme hygiene, a non-

place, imagination

obliterated, hired and blank

environment

bar area 24/7 without

human

         contact

or content, ultimate management solution

without person or persons

unknown, service

movement activated with a staff

of one

At Table Eight

boning up on Lowell's re-heat of history

Notebook 1967-68 and *Notebooks* (1970)

bent double over the table to mark the moment

where the siren enters the poem from the Real (left-hand margin in this case

its warning

a series of grey shapes

yes . . . no   yes . . . no   yes . . . no

what would you take to the next

life, being dead can't be more difficult

than before one was

born   then there's Mr Montage, Table Eleven

woman in the front row

ZEROSEVEN

I

difficult to settle

three electric storms one after the other, mid-

morning   BOOM   BOOM   BOOM

mobile cuts out   intermittent

contact /

       coverage the whole p.m.

don a waxed coat to keep the showers off

and dripping trees

            air cleared / green *is* green

yellow yellow   leaves, grasses, flowers

       re-calibrated   known, new

747 American Airlines passes low, shadow blotting the sun man-made eclipse

       to catch up on broken

            / sleep

exhaustion of years

later: Stan home possible job in architect's office

later still: listening over to 'Feedback,' the first mix

and 'Whistable Solo', the blood from Evan's sax

to the blood thru the ears   boom, boom, boom,

thru the stars

                        by eight   "live"

Michael Buerk and the panel putting Syria to rights

II

where one thing

becomes another thing   (note

to the memory   sight the sites

site the sights, the dual

prop dirge

of the plane overhead   (a music

of sorts to the conversation on the street below overheard

a street full

with sound, tipping

bottles to re-cycle, find a new

unfound form

work my way from the blue contour of motorway to work

and back like a vein mid-afternoon

txt from (silly) Siri canceling our Happy Hour cocktails

just as well

a bit of a relief if the truth be known, coming to light

in the day's light unfolding me

dyspeptic, morning and afternoon

the police siren trumpets

tempts me out to Town

and the point of the day

to step out later, find dinner and a drink

so to the Sea Cow for tuna, a glass of Sauvignon

and some level of racial abuse from the life of another

whose outlook is probably worse

III

blue jersey discarded on the bed

my attention pulls up alongside

I'm reading Blackburn's 'the black binder'

on what's fast become an admin day

sitting up in the Lloyd Loom chair

unnumbered Beings pass overhead

already halfway to the angels

vapour trails marking their spot

Speed Stick ($4.99) on the dresser

pops up for the memories of LA

beside my one desire to have you home

as Donald Byrd's *The Best of* pirouettes

the turntable and next door

'thank you for your call, Antigone'

26 POEMS: CALIFORNIALAND IN WINTER

(2014)

When a man dies his ideas are archived; but the key to the archive and the archive itself are lost.

—Ramón Gómez de la Serna, trans. by Guy Bennett

Solo – in Memory of His Father

climbing the thermal

stairway out of Manston

then immediately down

and across to Schiphol

shoved about by blocks of air

through milky cloud

three weeks since

my father's final hours

chased by who knows what

out of God knows where

into nowhere peering out

of pure blue

eyes one last confusion displaced

without knowing it

final R.E.M. muscle spasm

morphine nightmare

oxygen mask filmed with misty breath

cutting into the bridge of his nose

held from behind the head

a rubber band

as though strapped into his bed

for launch not quite ready

for the exact fit

the death mask always pure

blue above cloud cover

buried last Tuesday

9th February 2014

Amsterdam

1.

held over 'til the next day

in air

time for still

mineral water and strawberry waffle complimentary

the Fokker 70 Cityhopper crew

are in a line of air-blue uniform

bused route 197 Airport to Marnixstraat

spot 'Byzantium' – ideal for city centre car parking –

in transit → L.A. eighteen/nineteen hours

[insert two hours of sleep here]

after a ham and cheese toastie in the *Chaos* bar

accompanied by a strong whiff of skunk

and a saunter about the newly refurbed Rijksmuseum

to take in row on row of tourists and connoisseurs

swivel video and snap

Rembrandt's early self-portrait

'The Syndics'

upset the steady pouring of Vermeer's 'The Milkmaid'

transaction/image/information capture

traded for a closer   L   O   O   K

2.

the Bar of the American Hotel for "Geneva' martinis

stroll over the Singelgracht and back to Le Festa

pizza pasta red wine 40 Euros and the rest

anonymous elephantine stomping across the floor above

much laughter could get irritating through the night

ring stain left by a mug of tea

its okay I can take thirty-six hours without Outlook

Facebook – the delicate tea

the UHT milk sweet and heavy –

eye sockets purple with stress

dirt from my feet introduced

to the fresh bed linen

I lie down on and in

shrouding voices about my head

echo the street

from Hazenstraat 64

the clatter of sit-up-and-beg bikes

over cobbles below

9-10th February 2014

Arrival/New World

the 747 change of direction

yaws left around accelerated storms

the diverted Jetstream

and my father

teacher husband amateur restorer compiler of family histories

'your/flying coffin suspended between heaven and earth'

the days Blackburn passed through Amsterdam

turning over events these thirty/thirty five years gone

Cambridge   Oxford   London   Bethlehem PA

you visited 52   my age now

today is Monday 10th February 2014

jet above Greenland below the clouds like ice floes

bumpy over Canada in the race towards the land of movies

take another piss (fourth this flight)

three hours and seventeen minutes to Los Angeles

three hours and seventeen minutes of boredom

and all of the hours and all of the minutes

my father would trade to be bored

for one minute one hour on this flight

to be bored of me and all its strangers to be alive

10th February 2014

First Day in a New World

towards 11.ii.14 at 500 m.ph. +

somewhere over North Dakota nowhere

Casper Wyoming

Blackburn and the body that failed him

my father and the body that failed him

fully alive twenty-four hours today

$50 cab ride to Sunset

tip the driver another 10 bucks – a nice guy all the way

                                from Punjab

try to shop on Barrington for milk for tea

great dark void in place of concrete supermarket façade

shop for groceries on San Vicente in the end

miss black pepper miss garlic miss scourers miss

                                washing up liquid

they're in the schedule for another day

pass a lemon tree

full of lemons behind electric gates behind chain fence

this is Tuesday

11th February 2014 but I shouldn't need to tell you twice tho

11th February 2014

12th February 2014

1.

first shit since Amsterdam

I'm informing you Blackburn style

lizards skitter over cool Getty marble

the Western Fence Lizard

joust like knights bite chunks

ogling the sweetness

of portraits of jasmine of woman

Blackburn style in the manner of

Bernart de Ventadorn

'it is worthless to write a line

if the song proceed not from the heart'

or 'my dear and lovely friend, if ever

I come to have you in my power

and get into bed with you one night

and give you love-kiss, know it'

Beatritz de Dia

you totter along the marble plaza

balancing an Americano in one outstretched hand

and two glasses of iced water balanced

trapped between the fingers of your left

like the Virgin

or saint offering her heart

like the time you fell ill

the first time in silhouette

holding upright the saline drip

piped to your stomach

an emergency

like a figure from an altar

like a Venus

like a household goddess hair piled high

clutching a sheaf of corn or one of the Graces or

2.

we arrive the day Shirley Temple dies

where I'm asked for my username

there is nowhere to go

there is everywhere to go

'is Terri well enough to shop?

is Terri well enough to shop too?'

le Provencal condo on Barrington

walking passed 5.10 p.m. out walking

like taking a stroll at two a.m.

in the morning in real time

in the real time of my body

time delay backwards

to San Vicente Foods and back

12th February 2014

Out Walking

throw a grid over a desert like a Frisbee

and start the day with milky tea

feet plonked full-square beside the bed

bird-call like a cell phone alarm

and a nick to the throat

from shaving blossoms

rose-coloured blood

blooms and spreads so far

my father wouldn't recognise me for morphine

the act of memory close

closed into forgetting the act of memory

recede in the act of walking away

jay walking where elsewhere

walking is an art pleasure and gesture

an act of politics slowly

the act of flâneurism

the small man disappears into a crowd of them

morphing unidentified

a bird call the cadence of half

one side of a cell phone conversation

another winter afternoon fails into gloaming

he leans against the fence post at the graveyard

'where do you think you're going

you're mother's home's flooded on all sides'

13th February 2014

Sunday

a slow day

to the farmer's market on San Vicente

extra virgin olive oil picante 'Bella Rosalia

Marinara' – gifts for Elizabeth

the walk back to Sunset slow sun-kissed

lunch of guacamole pitta bread olives with Sandy

beneath shade beside pool

the pink walls of the courtyard green palms

leaning into that shade

time to attend to the routines and chores

brush teeth wash face

whilst shaving my father shoots the glance back

his lips forming into the question, 'why?'

I'm in the laundry fishing out a mix of shirts

underwear Flick's trousers a pair of jeans

its four weeks its as black and white as that

16ᵗʰ February 2014

Big Pink

there's been another day

a lunch of picnic and talk of how other days fell apart

the washing air-dries as the sun pitches

                                  downward toward 5.10 p.m.

a woodpecker hammers out the dusk just as jasmine unfurls

California sun heating the air stops like a thrown switch

late Sunday afternoon drag racing on the strip

Dodge Charger "v" Mustang GT

Bullitt (Dark Highland Green)

so nineteen-sixty-eight-Steve-McQueen

this Sunset sounds like the North Circular

all along the grid you know exactly where you are

navigating the anonymous familiarity of streets

where you don't lawns neat as Astro Turf

we walk on amidst a little too much reflection

from aluminum doors single glaze plate glass

standard issue crows and jackdaws calling

17ᵗʰ February 2014

100% Happy

never far off

a desert chill starts the day

and strawberry jam on multi-grain toast

from Peet's Coffee and Tea

corner of San Vicente and Gorham

the Staples All-Electric Truck opposite

'0% Exhaust 100% Happy'

sitting half shaded half not

the grass of the central reservation cultivated

look-alikey to Astro Turf but not –

the beds of blood-red flowers are raw mouths

the small man crossing

silence his private liberty his inheritance –

one life running to a stop

and I can't tell you the context only brush the surface

stumble over the pavement

a rough texture hot and cold to touch

come the day-lit or moonlit hours

24th February 2014

Pool

mid-Monday afternoon pool cleaning

foreign bodies netted lifted clear

of children's cries adults' murmur

the occupants on message for now

grainy as newsprint through bug screens

after the day's work the day's achievements

people understand in a minute the intention

lost intellect and ideas float free above

the Getty pool scene like *Death in Venice*

not the novel more the Dirk Bogarde Lido thing

smog at rest over L.A.

warm enough hummingbirds sip the flaming buds

where Immortality melts the sun flipped off

about six desert night chill

24th February 2014

Flâneur

lunch is

cheese burger fries shake from IN-N-OUT

on 5 north of Carlsbad after eighty miles

PER VEHICLE

2 OR MORE PERSONS

CARPOOLS ONLY

hawks circle the dunes and shoreline in pairs

                                    Apaches circle them

the dummy village three or four miles inland

you've got to watch out for the sign 'AWESOME' –

say what you need to say

salad leaves on the side

along the beach

checking the dates taste sweet or see

what works

worst case

Assault Craft Unit 5 like Swallows and Amazons

float up on skirts of air

eagles circle beyond that

Chevy Silverado white chrome grill sweeps past

CAMP PENDLETON U.S. MARINE CORPS

dunes Interstate 5 Rest Area shoreline ocean

24ᵗʰ February 2014

La Jolla Inventory

I

should have brought a thicker jacket

coffee off of the *Chalmers* stove

these chill mornings from the crest through binoculars

surf to horizon for grey whales migrating north for krill

                                    their dolphin escorts

top of the canyon a sandstone gully crows circling circling

and the shadows of crows

pretending to be hawks

call like crows tho

II

the thin blue-grey smoke of a cigarette wafts above

a trip to the Scripps Institution of Oceanography

and Aquarium for the leopard sharks

the full six foot brush past the legs

and the Eurotrash on La Jolla Boulevard

III

exit Extra Space Storage

dormant capacity

slow pick-up in the Car Pool

arrive for President's Day

the San Clemente city limit

to be taken in by the view

the crowd crowded the crowd

24th February 2014

Temescal Canyon

no access down Chautauqua no access

down Rivas Cyn Road

access so controlled for a country so free

off right to Skull Rock ahead Bienvenido

Trail left Viewpoint Trail

we follow Viewpoint Trail

and back along Sunset Trail

surrounded by serge scrub

California sagebrush California buckwheat

but the rattlesnakes aren't home

where the youth is pushing uphill

training all the way ahead

to keep fit and run down the hill

cartilage shot at the knee

the driest air voices crackle

home along W. Sunset Boulevard

tail-piped by a grey F12berlinetta

the scarlet Prius

this is what happens

if you buy a Ferrari in the wrong color

and this is the moral of our story today

27th February 2014

The Canyons

looking over to Santa Ynez out of sight and Topanga

the Santa Monica Mountains

my father dreams of my grandmother

dropping blackberries into the hollow

of the battered aluminum can c.1965

and its time for dreams of my father

turned away in silence face half

in shadow ox blood spot

on the side of his face spreading

roads head away from us and the Santa Monica Pier

land in the ocean beyond

Neil Young composing 'junk man

your mind is my invention' out there

time for Modelo beer

the sound of crows roosting like baboons

27th February 2014

94

Attention

sitting up in apartment #33 with dad

he's silent

(unusual for him

just me him and the Cadillac icebox

the bathroom area is sanitized

and you're eight hours ahead

of reality right here

the jackdaws think they're hummingbirds

and the rain is coming

this is an elegant table to work at

cherry or mahogany veneer

and I'm moving about its surface

why is air freshener more nauseating

than the stink of an overflowing toilet

27ᵗʰ February 2014

California

the alternator gone on the Kia Rio

and the toilet blocked –

what does it take

to block a toilet in California?

(one of those how-many- _____

does-it-take-to-change-a-light-bulb gags)

not much that's what

and the last DC-10 flew its last

last night so we'll all sleep easy enough tonight

and we've swopped the little metallic-blue Kia

automatic for a silver VW Jetta stick-shift

running slick and true

the thin veneer of concrete above

sand and red mud

27th February 2014

Human Scale

looking over the BBC schedule online for 'The Big Sleep'

somewhere to take the conversation elsewhere

whilst checking options for brunch

multi-task half-see

my father's fleeting profile

locked away in the freezing cold earth

here he's mute shadowed turned away

cutting into the organic bread like chopping wood

this organizing of materials

whose presence dissolves

feels like my abandonment

a grey L.A. day barely 16°

rain tipping down into the Hockney pool

I'm telling you everything I know

28th February 2014

Superba

there are no Commons in L.A.

but there are black Audi A5s

one on a tow truck stopped

the junction of Barrington and Sunset

a chunk ripped out of the near-side fender

all the Latinos maids gardeners say 'hello'

and await the Big Blue Bus

where's the sunny face

my father the man of the crowd

I pick a street and drive it

Wilshire Lincoln Boulevard

the crowd of trucks buses

SUVs sports coupés sedans

to watch his image dissolve

28th February 2014

Vancouver

7.23 the last few minutes

the sun's up

chilly boarding the plane

condensation at the glass

there has been rain

between Miriam dropping me off

security   immigration   duty-free

(should have bought that bourbon for C$20

sausage biscuit and sugared black coffee at Tim Hortons

then the long hop down the coast to LA for lunch

inner discourse seamless with Self

Radical Affections bookmarked with a napkin

from WestJet above Mount St Helens

giant cup of snow and firebreaks through the forest

beyond the horizon even at 37,000 ft.

mudflats (or are they salt flats?

lunar at this acute an angle

steep and away westward

wide fields and large plots

the 737 blown along

six minutes ahead

of its schedule

to LA and lots of books of poetry

eyes adjust

clearly signs

beat and voice

what a place

to receive J.J.'s

Songs In Midwinter For Franco

'to know how

to continue

in remembrance or not at all

smiling in slow motion

nothing special

in this fleeting

January day

worse month of the year'

my father more present than my wife

a late and last child

a last presence

a silent glass

upon a table

14th March 2014

Sunset

walking not driving this stretch of Sunset

11781 to 11461

'cross now' the white man sez

against the driver of the white Lexus

turning right on red

I clock a stain of mayonnaise on the right

leg of my 501s dropped from tomato

and salad last Thursday now bright and clear

and a warm breeze means a hot day

on the sidewalk the sign

'Open Hole Do Not Remove'

and the broken glass on brown concrete

and the city rooftops made of charcoal

and the walls of houses made from pastel

and the day's study

starting with Pollock's 'Mural' at the Getty

for ten minutes daily

the left-hand gallery for factory and circus

the place of work and leisure c.1950

Léger's drawings 'Happiness'

'The Acrobats' 'Circus'

my watch-face luminous against the sky

blue sleeve of my jacket

bright California day misty by 1.30

the Mexican worker hoovers leaves

and the Mexican men planting trees

at the close of the day shadow defines dark

14th March 2014

The Order of Things

time to scribble away at Time

as iced water melts its recycled cup

me woozy as the death of Mahler

the blood emptying from hands and feet

how people are missed/mourned

by the blue pool

in the pink courtyard

Jane gentle voiced and gentler smile

news of another away to the shadows

in this world of admin done

laundry done ATM card activated

in this world of earthquakes at 6.20 in the morning

and 5% chance of the 'big one' for three days to come

time to scrub away at dishes

for coffee and banana

the walk along West Sunset down Barrington

across Chenault fed into Westgate met at San Vincente

shop for groceries then the same in reverse order

the sun pouring endless

in the bleakest shadows

19th March 2014

11781 W. Sunset Blvd. Reprise Reprised

writing poems I'm sat here

ticking boxes meeting targets

sipping latte reading John James'

Songs In Midwinter For Franco

nothing better to do on the Getty

terrace except read Blackburn's

translation of *Poem of the Cid*

which I should be doing

fetched up found a spot

pass *Sunset West*

the white Getty bus judders passed

towards sunset and Apartment #33

11781 W. Sunset Blvd.

to guzzle down Cerveza Tecate

and reflect on Pollock's 'Mural' today's viewing

and Wednesday's 10.50 a.m. was better than T.V.

the teacher declared

we continue in our resolution to spend

a little of everyday with this picture marching across the wall

we do do we

19th March 2014

Towards

notes for appearing lost to

and shadow of eucalyptus at the window

of a certain pointing towards now

flecked dust to my eye

this is what March looks like

pool inked in shadow

father at a loose end

around midnight

like a waiter waiting on a tip

its nothing a little Bourbon can't fix

banking towards daylight and memory

holding his hand warm this one last time

sat in the upright position

Alaska Airlines 703

the seat in its upright position

the 737 trip a little bumpy along the spine

the Cascades towards Oregon towards Washington towards B.C.

steal an hour's nap heading north sun behind cloud or island

ocean   mountain   plateau

21ˢᵀ March 2014

Californialand in Winter

father farther out with each act

of memory whilst I'm here

locked between the non-stop grind of trucks west

and endless gridlock east

trying to learn Italian

from reading Franco Beltrametti's *Face to Face*

each neighbourhood a tight packet of stuff

far into the night where yesterday

your smile transforms history

and our sense of Being not merely economic

exchange from where I'm lying

the traffic thru my head

crunched thru voices of automobiles

further jolt at 7.20 p.m. further

time to breathe in California

bottom of ocean of air

25th March 2014

Poem Beginning and Ending with Today

today the day where yesterday your smile was

thirty years ago I received the news I'd be off

to Pennsylvania and so the journey begun

this drive La Jolla→LA north on Interstate 5 hop across I-405

101 miles to Quincy Jones' house on Santa Monica Blvd

Eames chairs and ottomans and gin and tonic

the day you returned from Gatwick cried your eyes out

in the bath after driving halfway round the 25 home

to where my feet stomp down the Californian dirt today

26ᵗʰ March 2014

Goodbye, La Jolla

tires over concrete slabs click like horses' hooves

cold running water from the faucet like frying

these are the Californian similes

thought up on the house balanced

at the edge of light

of heavy teak sliding doors of horizontal

light against the Pacific tilted high

blue air eucalyptus Scots pine up the coast

the guy who owns Walmart owns the huge palace

on the hacienda theme tipped

over boiling surf

he must enjoy the risk

to his booty

I pick a Bill Evans CD

'Alone' from the stack for translation

thru the Technics Compact Disc Player SL-P300

via the Bose Model 901 Active Equalizer

and Marantz Stereophonic Receiver Model 2245

of fidelity and felicity to the human ear

whilst outside pelicans float past to roost

26th March 2014

THE F TRAIN

(2014)

for Barry Schwabsky and John Yau

'*we're at Ocean Parkway now, 10-*
storey brick prisons, apartment houses, the parkway
W. 8th, the baths, Sophie's Corset Shop,
Rabinowitz's Pharmacy, Ruby's Fabric Center,
roofs all the way to the gas works
CAR   WASH   99¢
Stillwell Avenue   .   O fine,
end of the line   .   Coney
sun   .'

    — "At Prospect Park," Paul Blackburn

Delancey Street, May Twenty-First Twenty Fourteen

as Time slips over the electric-blue

watch face

to emerge at Delancey and Essex

in sight of the Williamsburg Bridge

the singing all the way thru

the truck backs up

like a message alert from a Nokia

all along Ludlow St.

the rising scent of baking pizza dough

the striking of metal tool against brick

the off-tone ringing

writing as 'magical' 'unmediated'

amid amassed documentation and data

content v disclosure

the thought of Walter Benjamin played out

night after night under neon

            INBORN
            TATTOO
            NYC

the morning opens off the Holloway Road

the evening closes on the Lower East Side

26th May 2014, Memorial Day

Storm

sitting in 81 Ocean Parkway the perfect place

reading *BROOKLYN-MANHATTAN TRANSIT:*

A Bouquet for Flatbush and 'Brooklyn Narcissus'

the rain swept along Church Ave. then down Coney Island Ave.

following other men's tracks

when will you follow your own

the man said above the storm

of flickering light and thunder

the sound changes the traffic

the traffic chucks up rainwater

over thru about walkers walking the sidewalks

the truck changes gear

throws more

cold water up

down and thru the body

the air close and warm

no question to mop or drip

too wet so sit the storm out

26ᵗʰ May 2014, Memorial Day

Hang a Left

the anything-goes-everything-must-go ideology

knowledge modeled in its management

o syrupy narcissi

o plague of anthologies

o plague on anthologies

as they parade so much weight

thru the Shinto mausoleum

look on into mirrors

mirrors look on into

the day the Macintosh building burned

what sad omen

the F train uptown to the Whitney Biennial

spring out of the subway

hang a left then hang a left

at the head of the stairs

worth it for Stuart Davis' 'The Paris Bit' (1959)

not in it

utopian *and* materialist

blue and white mainly

black and red a little

street scene and interior

still-life *and* landscape

UKIP Front National Golden Dawn

by Sunday all Europe jostled to the right

the Left didn't notice

while we weren't watching

et voilà — knowledge is made

history in its image

26th May 2014, Memorial Day

Memorial Day, Twenty Fourteen

is a rest day for the workers

a work day for the poets

the sun beaming away outside

bodies sprawled and smoking across Prospect Park

families of many races and one nation

their barbeques we step among them

to forget the apartment's gloom

pictures held to the wall by piano wire

all aspects of the East

the twenty-four hour landing lights

endless halls overlook one more endless

one apartment block mirror to the next

apartment block

echo of art deco for blocks echo

the cries of babies along landings

the cries of cats down landings

down stairwells that sound like cries

babies' cries that are cats' cries

down hard shine of mint-green bathroom tiles

down hard reflection on white subway tiles

down down down this yomi this Hades

28th May 2014

The 'F' Train

waiting for Labor Day propped against the Zinc Bar

my cogitation derailed by your change of Facebook status

as crimson melds into purple leads me astray to distraction

losing the will to scarves of chiffon sheets of satin shimmy air

air thinnest of vanities with tinny mirrors without attendance

my dad's the blue-faced Seiko the modern face of Japan

tells the days in French and today's day is Vendredi

rightly signed off where I am forever

and for life reach today the beginning of summer

this Memorial Day clean and sober

without me touching a thing my white iPhone

(assembled in China) has updated to 'Just Now'

28th May 2014

Lunch Poems

is fifty years old today

and the Puerto Rican cabbies

now are Indian Bangladeshi Chinese

$30 the fare (with tip)

W. 4th St. to Ocean Parkway

a GMO protest and a NYC bar

up and around NYU

Monday morning's quarterbacks

an EU earthquake the morning after

surf Facebook to blog to web page

to Richard Baker's 'Frank O'Hara's *Lunch Poems*'

at the Tibor de Nagy Gallery 2014

and the 50th anniversary edition in hard cover

intro by Ashbery afterword by Ferlinghetti

walk the morning Brooklyn grid for coffee

to the Nine Chains bakery

or home and tea the black Japanese

kettle with its bamboo handle

spits like a cat these are the choices

long after the neon fly-blown

ziggy-zaggy fire escapes rust away

the pink-purple brick green plane trees

reading Blackburn's *Proensa* in Prospect Park

starlings and chipmunks all fuss

the plane trees more fuzzy in Brooklyn

direct treatment of 'thing' Dr. Williams

28th-29th May 2014

Church Avenue

*Now I want the old man with white hair and glasses to cross
the road . . . come on, quickly . . . look this way . . . now
walk on to the left . . . ok, fine . . .'*
   —John Smith, from *The Girl Chewing Gum* (1976)

The Journals in the Nine Chains

one coffee one sauerkraut and corned beef

this Jeudi the air conditioned air a little

like fresh air coffee and cherry brownie

Vendredi adds up to a continuing habit

the guys from Mexico play dominoes

the corner of E7St. garage sale Jeudi

Vendredi corner opposite for the shade

hunched scrape and concentrate

white plastic tables chairs over concrete

the air sweats in Flatbush like roses or lilies

I listen to Radio 4 online to keep in touch

the bug screens and grimy panes

whine and clatter a Brooklyn overture or suite

rationing cat treats as tranquilizers

the girl walking the black and white terrier

parades "I DELETED TOM" in white letters

on a black t-shirt flashed across her chest

the guy wearing the "LA SISTER" t-shirt

behind so I cross to the sidewalk opposite calm

biographers are like private dicks

but I'm not writing the biographies

of the girl who deleted Tom or the man

whose sister resides in LA instead

I note parked the sixty-four Dodge Dart

the car the property of the Mexican guys

primed in battleship grey for re-spray

red wheels red interior additionally I note

however the truck of the National Dust

Control from Middlesex New Jersey

"LA SISTER SISTER SISTER"

insistent the monika as glimpses

of Manhattan Brooklyn dirty old air

sirens and yellow cabs running along

Ocean Parkway cats held in bad odor

crossing Prospect Park towards the end

of day fetch Palermo Extra Virgin

Olive Oil imported by Cosmopolitan

Food Group inc. Hoboken NJ 07030

Product of Spain to cook with to drizzle

above a street me sitting above

cats and cats like a mess says

Edwin Denby and keys tinkle

like dog-tags (foreground) honking

geese and trucks (background)

waiting on the laundry waiting

the utility basement floor grey

marked light bulb by light

bulb space utilized the washing

machine 'BUSY' clothes flickering

meeting with Allen

and Edith in the spirit

of some-things-are-better-

not 'hey come on up' P.B. hollers

from a window above decades ago

like writing a postcard home

in the early hours but not

I've a laptop and it's the moonlight

shifting and the streetlight

branches and leaves off the ceiling

pop to the Whitney for a second look

'LINES THICKEN' the Stuart Davis

declares from the frame 'The Paris Bit'

1959, and 'FRONT' and 'SMITH'

from 'House and Street' 1931

the trip to the Lesley Heller

Workspace 'this music crept by

me upon the waters' continuous

with the walk across Brooklyn

Bridge comfort and present

81 Ocean Parkway the block

constructed c. 1937 red

brick and pale green tile

living between elevator

and basement between

Westminster Road the Camero's

sound system BOOMS SO LOUD

summer air vibrates alters molecules

down this canyon of a street triggers car

alarms one after the other and the next

ah the little darlings don't need to go to NYC

to write like Frank O'Hara there's one in every town

in Philadelphia there's always been the 'Young Girl

Seated at a Virginal' 1670-2 and a tangle of street

signage boys and girls straw pork-pie hats tattoos

picking our way through Prospect Park

Flick at a trot to see Jonathan and Nick

the Brooklyn Museum on a bright

oppressive day all the better for the Rembrandt

'Self Portrait with Shaded Eyes' (1634)

or lunching with James at Emporio

on Mott off East Houston then on to Spring

and Mulberry with Flick in the hunt

for the perfect 'A' line dress F train

home in black with white polka dots

dinner at the Wheated on Church

service by Scott G I agree to pay

the above total amount pursuant

to the card issuer agreement for pizza

salad sparkling wine and celebration

Paul Blackburn Joan Blackburn

and Carlos T 'hello!' there they go

intercontinental the Gaucelm

Faidit Uzerchemobile putters along

in its own time to its own time

between Caton and Church

on McDonald the Pitta Funeral Home

and Pet Haven next door

taking the air to the Albermarle

Deli for three American pints of Modelo

Barry says he's free anytime

Charles can spare an hour stretches

an afternoon Miles can do lunch

but with Vivienne in tow

John makes very fine pork roast

30ᵗʰ May – 27th June 2014

Riding the F Train

Brooklyn's dirty old air keep an eye out

for the Window King security camera

corner of Caton Ave. and E.7th St.

to pick up the day's groceries in the One Stop Market

returning from Manhattan getting lost

around MacDonald Ave. and Church

is not a good idea a day before

but the beer's cheaper cooler more drinkable

having met Paul and Carol all the way north

in Glens Falls, forty miles out of Albany about

four hundred mile round trip via Penn Street Station

Fort Hamilton Parkway to change at Jay St. Metrotech

or to meet Mark a couple of days before that

rendezvous 243 Bleecker Rocco's pastry shop

then The Cornelia Street Café Trattoria Pesce

Pasta for soft shell crab and blue fish

Flick violently ill in Washington Square

then a yellow cab home (I blame the blue fish)

no metropolitan gloss to that emergency

bodies and events crushed together

into days' work

getting lost on Church Ave. is no good idea

3rd June 2014

Transcontinental

you arrive close to midnight London time

a life full of catnip and moult

to read places in sequence

a little pasta with hot sausage will do

playing into the cats' paws

oblivious to the bug screen and grubby panes

change at Jay St. Metrotech (again)

in Hollywood terms we are locked

between *Angel Heart* and *Barton Fink*

and I speculate you've stopped arriving there

this evening the sunshine strong

pouring down the air

the angry raised voices

construction workers

all along Coney Island Ave.

what looks like a Kia

stuck in the left-hand lane

off-side wing peeled back

like a can lid

woman driving still behind the wheel

8th June 2014

Morning, Flatbush

getting this down in a way I can't sleep dawn

in between feeding two cats

5.15 a.m. and break off —

I slept well — 10.50 a.m. now consult *The Journals*

I just wanted to see how it would appear

on paper in new light

opened at 'DECEMBER JOURNAL : 1968'

when father is no longer the memory's home movie flicker

he's traveling faster than light

that's all he is and that's all I know to add

to today's report filed this afternoon's activity

streets tangle signage around one

like a cigarette stubbed burns out the light of 16mm

I might as well be walking

Spring Street 1984 as walking Spring

Street 2014

hand on shoulder

the present continuous continues

10th June 2014

Corner of E. 10th and Church Avenue

can you pack more butter into that muffin

from behind the counter

reading Blackburn 1971 very active

that June his end drawing close

closed off poem by poem opened

into *The Journals* from *Halfway*

Down the Coast here the coffee's good

at a buck seventy-five from the high stool

he's moving faster than light I know

the angry voices and sirens far below

its Hades and the NYPD the FDNY

red fire truck pulls up

engine "Pride" 147 gaffered down the side

where there's no feeling left

like it turn in the thought

turn in the note turn in

the mother and daughter outside

sunning on the pink wooden bench

where leisure meets workspace

pleasure meets function where song

finds itself in protest of the street

not where's he's gone

there's nothing to be done

11ᵗʰ-12ᵗʰ June 2014

Hudson

I

brilliant early morning sunlight

along the river valley 160 miles north to Albany

town to cliff to river to forest all the way

reading the Hudson gives Blackburn's *The Journals* a rest

construction never stops no never the mighty cranes of Komatsu

digging north of the tip of Manhattan north of Inwood

first stop Yonkers empty as Bolton

wrecked warehouses walls and roof panels

missing graffiti the deep channel scraped glacial

thru Elysium to Tarrytown the abandoned GM plant

the Amtrak skirts the Hudson for an hour

Penn Station to Rensselaer

as the car fills with passengers the guy in the next seat

hunkers down to his Sony DVD

Sons of Anarchy at nine in the morning

where I'd draw the line draw back from scotch

the slide thru Paradise river left lagoon right

hour to hour the great blue herons flap pool to pool

II

train delayed Albany thirty minutes

head full of PB lunch and afternoon

with Paul and Carol and reflection

the boarded WAREHOUSE at Poughkeepsie

foraging starlings among dandelion clocks

the slope in sunshine towards sundown

plovers silos mills row boat halfway

to the lighthouse on the river estuary

and bulrushes for miles slow freight cars

two miles maybe two and half

trundle the western shoreline opposite

containers to the MAERSK Line

pull the top off a Dogfish Head IPA

9% proof specialty beer and sip

nuclear power-plant plus containment

the western shore

to Penn Street Station and final stop

12th June 2014

Lunch Follows Dinner

pigeon flops up onto the fire escape

fuzzy behind bug screen

one quart of Corona for the pleasure of it

and an omelette bacon in a muffin

people walking standing and sunning

people sitting eating and sunning

fresh from the One Stop Market

its 86° in Brooklyn

thirteen nights so far

and there's an ugly smell of burning

like Brixton of the 1980s

up and down Church Ave.

some Jamaican accents

hearing Spanish all day

reading Lorca in Blackburn's version

another late lunch at Nine Chains

another coffee at a buck seventy-five

there's a piece of grit to trouble my eye

across the room the pot sputters the refill

looks like half a cup then

then the deluge when

it rains in Brooklyn it rains

14th June 2014

Philadelphia

the Amtrak pulls through Trenton

a neighbor resting on the stoop

takes a smoke the long drag

leaning over a fire escape another

on my way to meet George

and marking my return

headphones held together with Meccano

like the freeways and railroad

a red cardinal flips the trash

the shanty town of north Philly

more temporary than thirty

years ago iPhone off seven hours

nothing much happened in Facebook land

the same trailer park truck stop row houses

—thirty years—all freeways streets railroads

lead to Newark New Jersey

derelict factory depot billboard torn down

14th June 2014

Downtown/Uptown

outside rain sounds like parcel tape dragged off the roll

and I can't really talk because I can't really think

at the end of the table there's a cup of tea half-finished

part of yesterday's schedule was to catch the Q train to the Guggenheim

I leave the bed cross the room to the desk

collect John Yau's *Further Adventures in Monochrome*

return to the bed all in the day's travel this is midtown

thinking *Breakfast* would be a good name for a poetry magazine

to reflect on the minute I saw the Rembrandt 'Self Portrait

with Shaded Eyes' (1634) that hour that afternoon that day

week month year all the seasons press in to rest with the seeing

a Penske rental truck occupies the street halfway up for the afternoon

stretched into evening at a push yellow and reflecting sunshine

the corner of the street in shadow a girl is skipping alone

19th June 2014

Midtown, a Friday

heading towards MOMA for four and its free entry

start at Fort Hamilton Parkway

go catch the Polke show for a dose of 'Capitalistic Realism'

uptown a few blocks from

R
A
D
I
O

C
I
T
Y *Music Hall*

crowds crowding about for the Dave Chapelle gig

the limousine style of the Rockefeller subway

at 47th-50th Streets like a Castro ZIL or GAZ

the taxis of Havana down the Avenue of the Americas

the scent of Halal from the street takeaway

for visitors hungry turned out at eight

the line halfway along W.53rd St. the crossing

flashes 4 3 2 1 seconds to cross and we do

its 73° in 34% humidity 5% chance of rain

20th June 2014

Chelsea

buying the A line skirt in the Gap

opposite The Chelsea Hotel

it's the Saturday after Friday

the thirteenth and all the more reason

to write a poem then

with me hanging around outside

changing rooms awaiting your verdict

at my wrist his self-winding watch

dead as a stone

its poor time-keeping and the thought of him

leaves me the blues and reflection

sworn on my grief no more looking back

as the blue Toyota Echo follows the Yellow Cab

turning right on red

we stride out along W. 23rd St.

a couple of preppy boys

rush by looking like an Alex Katz

towards a snack metamorphosed

into dinner of pate and cheeses a halfway decent

house red the cabernet raised in Santa Cruz

at the Trestle on Tenth

24th June 2014

Sunday, Sunday

the lunchtime change of venue

to 'The Lark' and about a page

the image timed out it's a rainy Sunday

then on to Santos Anne 366 Union Avenue

'G' train to Metropolitan Avenue

for dinner and conversation

return to the prison blocks of Ocean Parkway—

not that late and ready

to drink the wine off the plane

Château Moulin de Honternieux Médoc 2012

poorly kept in plastic bottles

next on the shelf

a snazzy choice of preserves

relaxing beside the midnight freeway

a pool of pop lyrics wafted up

above the side street construction site

storm ending blip blip blop

26th June 2014

The Blue Note

light bulbs *are* a pleasure at midday

as Frank O'Hara conjured Edwin Denby

saying from the middle of the floor of this sitting

room of this dark and purple apartment

(purpled not from red wine) where the watch stops

if I stop moving (if it stops will I stop

remembering?) here the aircon is full

blast like being aboard a mid-Atlantic zeppelin

and my wallet's here where I've scooped

nickels dimes and pennies for five weeks

where I've fantasied those five weeks

after a halfway decent bottle of red

with no liquor store for ten or fifteen blocks

between Modelo and Beaujolais

somewhere my Achilles Heel

head lost in the quiet cool objective past

its getting kinda late and its time

to enter a new space entire

wring me out with handprints

27ᵗʰ June 2014

Seen from the 'Q' Train

the 'Spirit of America' chugging along to Staten Island seen beyond

Brooklyn Bridge traffic bikes and pedestrians helicopter below

Statue of Liberty above

next stop Canal Street

NYC a faster city c.1985

or the memory plays its tricks

a lighter sense of air and sunlight

to its substance its only memory

car alarms set off by thunder

the parked cement trucks and vans

behind chain-linked fence

commerce done for the night

beyond the grey misted window

thru these objects the shadows' light

pinky hue light-grey the edge

of the luminous

the blue impossible sky beyond

the dad who died of the cure

27ᵗʰ June 2014

146

Free Verse Editions

Edited by Jon Thompson

About the Author

Simon Smith has published five collections of poetry. His third collection, *Mercury* (Salt Publications), was long-listed for the Costa Prize in 2007. A selected poems, *More Flowers Than You Could Possibly Carry*, appeared from Shearsman Books in 2016, and his latest pamphlet is *Salon Noir* (Equipage, 2016). Peter Riley recently wrote essays on his work for *The Fortnightly Review*. Smith is Reader in Creative Writing at the University of Kent, was a Hawthornden Writing Fellow in 2009, and a judge of the National Poetry Prize in 2004. He holds a PhD from the University of Glasgow.

Photograph of the author by Felicity Allen. Used by permission.